Who Am I?

A Simple Riddle, That When Solved, Answers the Age Old Question We All Ask Ourselves...

Who Am I?

Argus Gray

Disillusionment Press
USA / WORLDWIDE

Copyright © 2016 by Argus Gray

Original Copyright © 2015

ISBN-13: 978-0692649572 (Disillusionment Press)

ISBN-10: 0692649573

All rights reserved. This book may not be reproduced in whole or in part, stored in a retrieval system, or transmitted in any form or by any means, electronic, mechanical, photocopying, recording or otherwise without the written permission of the author.

For those who not only ask …
but, also seek

the
riddle...

What **four** letters...

made up of **three** different letters...

spell **one** word when written...

sound like **four** words when spoken...

and forms **one** sentence...

that is the key...

to your **enlightenment**?

If you are using your **thinking** mind
to answer the riddle that is fine ...

but know this ...

the **answer** was given to you
before you even opened the **cover.**

The answer is ...

Wait...

Are you **sure you** really want to **know**?

I mean the **answer's so** absurdly **obvious**, **it's almost** embarrassing that I felt a need to write this **ridiculous** book.

Okay, okay—I get it ...

You want to know the answer.

So here goes...

Wait one more minute...

Wouldn't you rather spend a lifetime of **contemplation** on this spiritual riddle, instead of having the **answer** simply given to **you** in one of the shortest books you have ever read?

No.5

Alright then ...
the riddle,
and its **answer**,
is on the next page.

What **four** letters...

made up of **three** different letters...

spell **one** word when written...

sound like **four** words when spoken...

and forms **one** sentence...

that is the key...

to your **enlightenment**?

G. U. R. U.

I told **you** it was **obvious**.

In fact, it's so much so, you'd think the **Universe is** screwing with **us.**

Yes, **Guru** is a Sanskrit term for "teacher" or "master," but could this ***Universal inside joke*** be any more blatant then when actually speaking all four letters aloud ...

G-U-R-U

Yep, that's right ...

Gee, yo**U** a**R**e yo**U**.

So, now you know ...

There is **no need** to sit cross-legged chanting for hours on end.

There is **no need** to spend hundreds,
or even thousands of dollars
on self-help baubles.

There is **no need** to seek out wise, old yogis on distant Himalayan mountaintops ...

And, yes ... it also means there is
no need *to even read this book.*

Because there is **no need to learn,**
what you already **know.**

So, the next time you feel lost
and are **searching for** answers ...

gaze into your mirror and behold ...
your very own sacred teacher;

your GURU

staring back at you,
smiling ...

For **the answers you seek**

are not atop a mountain ...

.. they **are** within **you**.

About the Author

Argus Gray is the name given to
a boy who has never grown up.

Whether it's because he can't ...
or because he won't ... is still unknown.

His physical body resides in Upstate NY,
driving his beautiful wife, Lenore, nuts from
his A.D.D. and erratic mood swings.

The rest of him ...
lives happily in his own small mind ...

.. writing quick read books for an A.D.D. generation,
and telling stories to whoever will listen.

Also by Argus Gray

Did You Know "Richard Cory"?

Wake Up & Live!
How To Conquer The Rip Van Winkle Syndrome

Suicidal Thoughts

The Book of Truth
.. And Lies

If I Could Travel Through Time

Do You Know...
7 Simple Thoughts to Help You Awaken

Rubber Rocketship
A Very Short Story of Love, Loss & Eternity

Sleeping In The Trees
The Secret World of Princesses & Princes

Contact Argus Gray at:

www.argusgray.com

argusgray@gmail.com

Watch Argus Gray online at:

www.grayatnight.com

YouTube Channel: GrayatNight

www.ingramcontent.com/pod-product-compliance
Lightning Source LLC
Chambersburg PA
CBHW071313060426
42444CB00034B/2179